BREATHE IN
GOD
BREATHE OUT
ANXIETY

A WORKBOOK of EVERYDAY WAYS to FIND CALM

Dr. Matt Miller, PsyD

Andrews McMeel
PUBLISHING®

Andrews McMeel Publishing
a division of Andrews McMeel Universal
1130 Walnut Street, Kansas City, Missouri 64106

www.andrewsmcmeel.com

25 26 27 28 29 RLP 10 9 8 7 6 5 4 3 2 1

ISBN: 978-1-5248-9506-8

Editor: Jennifer Leight
Production Manager: Tamara Haus

ATTENTION: SCHOOLS AND BUSINESSES
Andrews McMeel books are available at quantity discounts with bulk purchase for
educational, business, or sales promotional use. For information, please e-mail the
Andrews McMeel Publishing Special Sales Department: sales@amuniversal.com.

CONTENTS

God cannot give us
a happiness and peace
apart from Himself,
because it is not there.
There is no such thing.
—C. S. LEWIS

INTRODUCTION

~~~~~~~~

IF ANXIETY HAS BEEN A THORN IN YOUR LIFE, you're taking an important first step by opening this workbook and preparing to bring your honest feelings to God. That feeling of fear, dread, and uneasiness in response to current or future stress-inducing situations . . . that's anxiety. And God wants it—and any other messy emotion you can think of. *All of it.*

Often, that truth seems hard for us to believe. Why would God want us to bring that all to Him? After all, He already knows anyway. Consider this: What if our expression of these concerns is not for Him, but for us? When we see it all laid bare, something a little frightening but wonderful often happens. Our hearts soften, and God begins to work in us. I've seen it time and time again in counseling sessions with people of all ages and backgrounds.

So where do we start when we feel like anxiety has sapped our energy, hope, and enjoyment to the point that we are running on fumes, our soul is so weary, and we'd love nothing more than to rest? We begin by asking God to help us see what's holding us back and all the good that's waiting for us on the other side of anxiety. Throughout my nearly thirty years of experience as a clinician and professor, I have helped people begin to understand the root causes as well as perceive the visible fruit of anxiety in their lives. The exercises in this workbook are designed to guide you in that process. They will help you uncover deep-seated fears while finding relief in high-pressure moments. Both are necessary paths out of anxious places.

As you progress through the units in this workbook, you will also come to see how recognizing anxiety can be a surprising blessing—a signpost that points us to our finiteness, weakness, and dependency. When everything feels like too much, our anxiety alerts remind us that we need to cling to our Creator and Father, who so dearly wants us to be near to Him. We find freedom in surrender as Jesus invites us to rest on His chest and experience Him as the one "who comforts us in all our troubles" (2 Corinthians 1:4). This is God's redemption at work. Not only can we have joy and intimacy with our Lord in spite of anxiety, but anxiety is transformed from a barrier to joy into a bridge where we can cross and meet with Him, and He with us. As we experience God in the midst of our anxieties, our misconceptions and projections of who we believe God to be fall away and are replaced by knowing God as one who is our Good Provider who loves us more than we may ever be fully able to fathom.

Take His hand and trust as He leads you day by day and week by week into the calm that only He can provide. God wants all the energy that is currently going into managing your anxiety to instead fuel meaningful relationships, joyful experiences, and neverending praise. May it be so!

GUIDELINES FOR GETTING STARTED

- + The units in this workbook will be most helpful if you work through them in order. But if a certain aspect of anxiety is calling out for immediate attention, follow the Spirit to that unit and then come back to the rhythm of the book.

- + It may work best to enter into a new unit each week, allowing a day to meditate on the introductory message and then a day for each of the three to five exercises, but feel free to honor the best pace for you. Some of us are waders, while others like to jump right in.

- + Always begin by asking God to open you to wherever He wants to lead you that day.

- + Consider beginning the workbook at the same time as a friend or even as a small group. You can walk through the units together and share as you feel comfortable.

- + Listen for any messages that come through and urge you to follow up with a pastor, priest, therapist, or counselor. These exercises are not meant as a substitute for a therapeutic relationship. God gave us counselors so that we don't need to do the hard work alone!

Know thyself, for once we know ourselves, we may learn how to care for ourselves.

—SOCRATES

CHECK
THE WEATHER

ONE OF THE FIRST THINGS MANY PEOPLE DO in the morning is consult the forecast. Will today bring sunny skies? Clouds? Rain? What's the temperature? Sometimes, that weather app or report is helpful; other times, you need to step outside and feel for yourself.

Experiencing emotions is a lot like checking the weather. It can be easy to approach emotions intellectually, like when you seek out that "expert" forecast. But it's only when you step outside and feel the sun warm your head, the wind brush your cheeks, or the rain trickle down your nose that you truly experience the weather. Likewise, emotions need to be experienced. Remember some of the most powerful words in the Bible: "Jesus wept" (John 11:35).

In the rush of our lives, finding the time to process emotions can be hard. Yet, throughout each day, you are likely experiencing a wide range of them. What happens when you feel something? Many people suppress feelings or push past them to get through the day. The problem is that we don't circle back to these feelings and they build up inside of us over time. That's not what God intends for us.

With the help of the exercises in this unit, you can begin to recognize what anxiety feels like for you. As you process your feelings and take care of yourself in the storms, you'll find more freedom to enjoy the sunny times when they come. That's honoring God's provision.

1

LISTEN TO YOUR BODY

PAUSE RIGHT NOW AND DO A BODY SCAN. Starting with your feet and working upward, focus on one body part at a time. Tune in to your toes, ankles, calves, knees . . . all the way up to your neck, jaw, eyes, and forehead. Notice how your body is feeling.

Do any particular places feel tight or tense?

_____

_____

Are certain areas easier or more difficult to feel?

_____

_____

Think back over your day. Can you connect any events to how your body feels at this moment? Example: "My neck feels that tense discussion with my sister." Don't try to jump to solutions; just note how anxiety touches you.

_____

_____

2

LEARN FROM A MEMORY

REVISIT AN EVENT in your life that is full of emotion. Whether that day felt like the loudest, scariest thunderstorm or the brightest of sunny days, reach back and write down every feeling it brings up right now. You don't even need to write full sentences (no grades here!). Not sure how to start? Try thinking about the experience through your five senses. The goal is not to linger in the past but to simply help you create awareness of your feelings.

_____

_____

_____

_____

_____

_____

_____

_____

3

FEEL A PSALM

"For we do not have a high priest who is unable to empathize with our weaknesses, but we have one who has been tempted in every way, just as we are—yet he did not sin."

—Hebrews 4:15

GOD CREATED EMOTIONS. God knows what it's like to experience the feelings we have. Many passages in the Bible speak to us on an emotional level. Special shout-out to Psalms! Pick one Psalm to read right now. As you read it the first time, put yourself in the writer's shoes and see what emotions you pick up.

Psalm read:
_____

What emotions come through from the writer?

_____

_____

Now, read it again, thinking of a situation in your life. What emotions come through for you? Are they different from or similar to your takeaways from the first reading? No worries about right answers! Awareness is the key.

_____

_____

_____

_____

_____

4

KNOW YOUR WARNINGS

While there are some common sensations, each person will have their own experience with anxiety. What triggers anxiousness for you and how that feels may not look the same for the person next door. This holds for any emotion. You can cultivate a more mindful approach to your emotions by becoming more aware of how you experience them.

ON THE THERMOMETER that follows, each number represents a level of anxiety, with one being the lowest level of anxiety and five being the most intense. In the space next to each level, jot down the physical sensations you feel and behaviors you typically engage in when you're experiencing that measure of anxiety. So, level two anxiety might feel like a slight tightness in the chest and irritation, whereas level five means a rapidly beating heart and the feeling that you'll collapse.

ANXIETY THERMOMETER

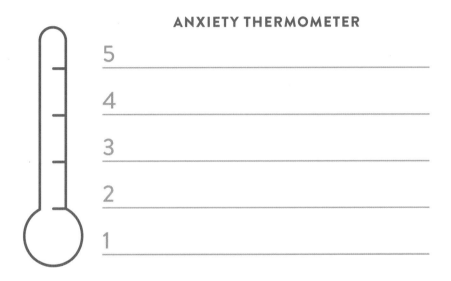

The goal is for you to practice differentiating between the levels of anxiety you experience to grow your awareness of yourself. Knowing your weather alerts can help you make informed decisions based on what you're feeling. If it looks, feels, and reminds you of rain, you better carry a raincoat—or whatever can bring you emotional shelter! Come back to your thermometer from time to time and update it whenever needed.

Feelings are
something you have;
not something you are.
—SHANNON L. ALDER

NAME YOUR FEELINGS

~~~~~~

ENDLESS WAVES OF EMOTIONS come and go throughout each day. They can feel so big and bundled that it's difficult to sift through each one and make sense of how you're feeling. It can also be tempting to define an entire event or day by one emotion because it felt so strong.

Whenever we're faced with something really powerful or challenging to take in, it helps to break it down into pieces or pictures we can understand. Isn't that how we begin to approach knowing God? In order to understand who God is, you have to look at all the information you have about His character. You may consider your knowledge from the Bible and how God has worked in your life and others' lives. To gain a deeper understanding of God, we may also use different names for Him—from Yahweh and Father to Creator and Comforter.

We can approach emotions in the same way. You can get to know them better by considering past experiences and giving them a name. By putting a name to what you feel, you increase awareness of yourself and can then make informed decisions based on what you're feeling. The exercises in this unit will help you start understanding and naming emotions in yourself and others.

1

SCHEDULE A MEETUP

Set alerts to check in with your emotions a few times throughout the day. Using the wheel on the next page to help, try naming your feelings. (You can search online for wheels that go even deeper into detailed emotions.) Even if you're not 100 percent sure, identifying emotions is a skill that improves with practice. It's like riding a bike! Notice the sensations in your body, consider what has happened today, and remember other times you felt this way. What emotion(s) might you be feeling? Be as specific as you can.

Check-in 1:

_____

_____

Check-in 2:

_____

_____

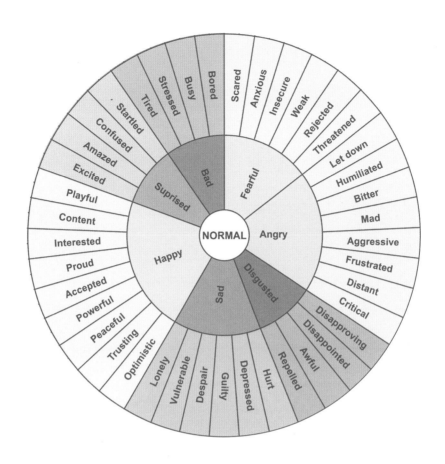

Check-in 3: _____

_____

_____

Check-in 4: _____

_____

_____

DISCOVER AN ARC

CHOOSE ONE PERSON IN THE BIBLE whose story is told with some depth over more than one passage. As you read through chapters and verses that include them, notice any words that indicate an emotion. How many different emotions do you pick up?

3

DRAW IT

PICTURES CAN SPEAK AS WELL AS WORDS. In the space that follows, illustrate what it feels like when you're anxious. You might sketch yourself as a stick person with signs that show physical sensations, the swirling winds of a tornado with lightning bolts, an impish monster wreaking havoc, or your brain filled with a jumble of thoughts—whatever image feels like the best expression of what you're feeling inside. Maybe you just need to color aggressively with a bright-red marker! There is no right or wrong—only the truth of how you feel when anxiety hits.

Each moment is
a choice. No matter
how frustrating or boring
or constraining or painful or
oppressive our experience,
we can always choose
how we respond.
—EDITH EGER

EXPRESS YOURSELF

IT'S OFTEN SEEN AS STRONG to keep emotions under the surface. But think of a beach ball that you keep pushing underwater. It takes a lot of effort and energy to hold it there. It could pop to the surface at any time when you let your guard down. Wouldn't it be better to deal with the beach ball on your own terms? Let it come to the surface, hold onto it, and deflate it if you like. Keep that picture in your head. That's why it's so important to find (healthy) release.

Jesus expresses His emotions frequently in the Gospels. When He was sad, He wept. When He was angry, He flipped tables. When He was exhausted, He took a break. When He was lonely, He called on God and His friends to be near. Jesus was able to feel all the emotions that we feel, experiencing humanity like us. The difference is that Jesus never sinned. Rather than suppress feelings or act out erratically, Jesus expressed emotions appropriately and honored the Lord.

The good news (well, the *other* good news): even in all of the human brokenness, you can find ways to express your emotions appropriately as well. Learning to identify your emotions sets you up to choose what to do with what you're feeling. You won't be caught off guard. For example, if you need to have a serious conversation with someone in your life, first step away from the situation and identify what you're feeling. From there, you can choose how to respond in a way that won't leave you feeling worse or harming a relationship you want to maintain. The exercises in this unit will help you express emotions in a helpful, constructive way.

1

PRAY OUT LOUD

"Trust in him at all times, you people; pour out your hearts to him, for God is our refuge."

—Psalm 62:8

FIND A QUIET PLACE where you can be alone. Once you're settled in your space, pour out your heart to God. Talk to Him about your feelings (all those swirling worries!) and the happenings of the day. Allow yourself to be open and expressive—even if it feels odd at first. Often, talking out loud helps express emotions more effectively than praying silently. How do you feel afterward? Is there anything that could make it easier next time? (One idea: Read selections from Lamentations.)

2

PINPOINT YOUR PEOPLE

"A friend loves at all times, and a brother is born for a time of adversity."

—Proverbs 17:17

THINK OF TWO PEOPLE IN YOUR LIFE with whom you feel safe—people whom you trust enough to talk to when life gets hard. Write their names on the lines below and include any notes about areas where they bring special comfort or knowledge. The next time you're experiencing an emotion and need help expressing it, reach out to one or both supports to talk through what's going on. Make them favorite contacts on your phone if they're not already. If you find yourself in need of more trustworthy friends, pray that you can meet the people God has for you. Then, be courageous and put yourself out there to meet those people.

1. _____

_____

_____

_____

2. _____

_____

_____

_____

TAKE ACTION

MAKE A LIST OF SAFE (even seemingly silly) ways to express overwhelming emotion. Examples: Punch a pillow, scream in an empty house, sing at the top of your lungs, pulverize some ingredients in the blender. Your goal is to help take the edge off of what you're feeling. Sometimes, having just a second to breathe and express yourself can make all the difference.

4

GIFT YOURSELF RELEASE

KEEPING EMOTIONS TRAPPED INSIDE just stokes their intensity. Anxiety, in particular, can feel like a spiral, with your thoughts circling endlessly and the worry only getting worse. To find the off-ramp, you need a regular practice of release. Buy a journal or sketchbook, whichever feels more natural for you. Then build up the habit of writing or drawing it all out. Here's a plan to get you started:

Journal or sketchbook?

_____

Designs/themes/colors to look for that will encourage me to use my outlet:

_____

Time and place that will work best for my practice each day:

_____

Environmental encouragement to include (for example, relaxing music, warm beverage, special pen):

_____

God gave us memory
so that we might have
roses in December.

—J. M. BARRIE

REMEMBER
THE ROSES

~~~~~~~

WE TEND TO FIND WHAT WE LOOK FOR IN LIFE. God is constantly at work in our lives and our world. If we look for signs of God at work, we will find them. Yet, many of us miss the signs. We have to train ourselves to see with different eyes. A significant reason why many of us struggle to see God at work is that we cease to remember what God has already done.

What have you done for me lately? We are not alone in forgetting what God has done. God brought the Israelites out of Egypt. He came through for them and protected them again and again. Yet, while Moses was away, they forgot quickly what God had already done for them. Fear and anxiety crept back into their lives. As we forget, like the Israelites before us, it allows lies about God, our lives, and our relationships to seep into our consciousness.

In this unit, you will be guided through exercises designed to correct your vision by improving your memory. Challenge yourself—with God's help—to tend the garden of your emotions and have roses in December.

1

CHANGE YOUR GAZE
TO PRAISE

*"Finally, brothers and sisters, whatever
is true, whatever is noble, whatever
is right, whatever is pure, whatever
is lovely, whatever is admirable—if
anything is excellent or praiseworthy—
think about such things."*

—Philippians 4:8

OUR DAILY FOCUS can lead us to different conclusions about how we see our lives and the world around us. Take Philippians 4:8 to heart. Start by writing down five things in God's creation that are "praiseworthy." Then carry the thought of these blessings and your "praise lens" with you throughout your day.

1. _____

_____

2. _____

_____

3. _____

_____

4. _____

_____

5. _____

_____

2

REFLECT ON THE ROAD YOU'VE COME

Just as what we see in a mirror is a reflection of who we are, so is our memory. When we look into a mirror, it should reflect accurately. If not, it has more in common with a carnival mirror. We've all stood in front of a carnival mirror that makes us look taller or shorter, makes our face look wider or thinner. Often, our memory is like that carnival mirror . . . distorted. As Christians, we have a struggle with anxiety that often includes only remembering the negative times and forgetting how God has been at work in our lives. Let's seek a more accurate reflection of God's grace, power, and love in our lives.

SET ASIDE TEN MINUTES to recall just one time you were aware of God at work in your life. Go deep into details. Try to remember your thoughts, feelings, and desires at the time. Be specific about the ways that God was at work. If you struggle to remember the details, take time to pray and ask God to help you remember accurately.

3

START A CIRCLE OF STORIES

"Some men came carrying a paralyzed man on a mat and tried to take him into the house to lay him before Jesus. When they could not find a way to do this because of the crowd, they went up on the roof and lowered him on his mat through the tiles into the middle of the crowd, right in front of Jesus. When Jesus saw their faith, he said, 'Friend, your sins are forgiven.'"

—Luke 5:18–20

OUR MEMORIES AND STORIES are not just our own. For example, you really do not remember falling into the cake when the birthday clown scared you on your second birthday. You "remember" it because your family has told that story over and over again. Our stories can help others. They can encourage, challenge, and, at times, make people laugh. When we tell our stories to others, they also become keepers of our memories. In the future, you may forget the story, but there is a good chance they won't. If and when that time comes, they will be able to encourage you. Over coffee, share your "Reflect on the Road" story from page 35 with a friend.

Whom did you share with?

_____

What was their reaction?

_____

_____

How did it feel telling your story—which is also part of God's story?

_____

_____

_____

_____

4

SEE YOUR ABUNDANCE

VISUAL REMINDERS HELP US to remember. Pictures in frames, ribbons pinned on a shirt, all those sticky notes *everywhere*. Creating visual reminders of God at work will not only help you to remember what God has done but will also help you to better see God at work in your present circumstances. All you need is a large jar and the beginning of a collection that will bring you joy.

Every time God answers a prayer in your life (or in the life of someone you love) or you see God at work, add to your jar. Your filler could be seashells or small stones, or even golf tees or LEGOs. Whatever you find pleasing to look at can work—as long as it isn't perishable! Keep your jar somewhere you will see it every day as a reminder of God at work. And be prepared to add more and more jars to your collection—God's goodness is overflowing.

POST A PHOTO (OR DRAW A SKETCH) of your jar and first additions here. Note the date you began the practice. If you'd like, share your photo on social media and tag it #Godatworkjar.

- -

Then the LORD God formed a man from the dust of the ground and breathed into his nostrils the breath of life, and the man became a living being.

—GENESIS 2:7

RECLAIM YOUR BREATHING

IN YOUR MIND, GO TO A CALM PLACE. Maybe it's the beach with soft, warm sand kissing your feet, the whoosh of gentle waves rolling in, and a hint of salt on your lips. Or it could be a shady hidden spot under a willow tree with whispering breezes and lilting bird songs.

As you pictured this scene, you may have noticed your body easing into a more relaxed place and pace as well. Your breathing likely calmed. When you are feeling anxious, your breathing rhythm and depth are typically the first stressed reaction. You may take shallow breaths, gulp for air, or even struggle to catch your breath. As your breathing gets more and more dysregulated, it signals your body that you're not safe right now, heightening the anxiety.

To move back to calm, settle your breathing. Think about how the ocean tides ebb and flow. The waves may grow and crash, but they keep their rhythm no matter what. It takes time for waves to build up enough water to crest, and then after they reach the shore, they must crawl back to the sea. If the water moves too fast, it's indicating a storm may be coming. Similarly, an anxious mind wants your body to heighten its responses to deal with a perceived threat. The breathing exercises in this unit will help you feel storms on the horizon and find a natural rhythm, just like waves.

PUT YOUR BREATHING IN A BOX

Let a simple square guide you in a powerful breathing exercise. As you trace a finger from left to right across the top side, inhale slowly and deeply through your nose for four seconds. When you turn the corner and continue down the second side, hold that breath for four seconds. As you move your way from right to left across the bottom side, exhale slowly through your mouth for four seconds. Heading up the final side of the square, hold your breath once again for four seconds. Continue around the square until you feel your heart and breathing have slowed to a relaxed rhythm.

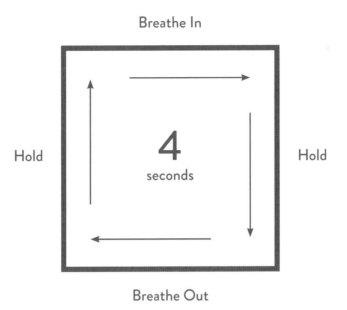

A few variations to try:

+ Picture a square in your mind to try this breathing technique anytime, anywhere.

+ Instead of counting to four, say a word in your head four times. It could be the same word (such as *God* or *peace*) all the way around or varying words for the inhales, holds, and exhales. Pencil in the word(s) near the box guide above.

FIND CALM IN FIVE FINGERS

HOLD UP YOUR NONDOMINANT HAND with your palm facing you. Take the pointer finger of your dominant hand and touch it to the base of your thumb, right by your wrist. Slowly move your finger up the side of your thumb, pausing at the top before running your finger down the other side. Continue up the side of your pointer finger, down the other side, up your middle finger, and so on. As you move your finger up, inhale through your nose. Whenever you move it down, exhale through your mouth. Keep going up and down over your fingers until you reach the other side of your hand, where you can either stop or move in reverse over the same pattern. Repeat as many times as you need. Let the pace of your movement guide your breathing to be slow, deep, and deliberate.

Was it easy or challenging to make it around all your fingers without losing focus?

_____

_____

_____

_____

GO TO THE OCEAN

WHEN YOU FEEL ANXIETY BUILDING, close your eyes and return to the calming image of the beach. Use thoughts of the waves to guide your breathing. Breathe in slowly and deeply through your nose as the water ebbs back into the ocean; breathe out deliberately through your mouth as gentle waves crash onto the shore. Continue this wave breathing as long as you need to slow a racing heart and find a path out of anxiety and into calm.

How do you feel after the exercise?

_____

_____

_____

_____

_____

_____

_____

_____

4

TAKE A BREATHER
EVERY DAY

Breath is life. God gave us the breath of life and created our bodies to function in specific ways. The *Yahweh* name for God even resembles the sounds of an inhalation and exhalation: "Yah . . . weh . . ." But as automatic as it seems, breathing is best practiced to get the most calming benefits. Every breath you take sends signals throughout the body—your breathing can take you into crisis mode or a relaxed state. The more you practice steering your breathing, the more time you can spend in that good place, enjoying all that God has placed in your life. If you practice regularly, the calming techniques will be readily available when you are feeling just a bit anxious or a real crisis hits.

SO MAKE A PLAN TO SLOW DOWN and practice a breathing exercise for a few minutes each day. As you enter into your quiet time, don't forget to dedicate your breathing to the Lord and ask Him to help guide you into calm.

Set-Apart Time for Breathing Practice

Monday: _____

Tuesday: _____

Wednesday: _____

Thursday: _____

Friday: _____

Saturday: _____

Sunday: _____

I see trees of green,
red roses too. I see them
bloom for me and you.
And I think to myself,
what a wonderful world.

—LOUIS ARMSTRONG

TOUCH THE GRASS

GOD HAS CREATED A VAST AND BEAUTIFUL WORLD.
From deep-sea microorganisms to the highest mountain peaks, the Creator is sovereign over all. God is revealed in His creation. By looking at the beauty and complexity of nature, you see the handiwork of the Lord. You can take comfort in a grand design and purpose and find hope and life in His hands. It's no surprise, then, that being in nature can help reduce anxiety. When you go outside and focus on nature, it can help you feel more connected to God and all of His creations, bringing a sense of calm.

But when life feels too busy or too crazy, we find it hard to pause and head into the great outdoors. In the grand scheme of our schedules, looking at plants and birds doesn't seem that important. Yet, spending time outside can have a significant impact on anxiety levels. Anxiety often gets you stuck in your head and focused heavily on yourself. It can be hard to think of others. Hold a leaf in your hand, feel the grass, and smell the flowers, and your focus will move outside of yourself.

In this section, you'll find some simple ways to engage with nature to reduce anxiety and help get your focus out of your head and onto your Creator.

1

WALK IN THE WEATHER

THE QUICKEST WAY TO GET FRESH PERSPECTIVE is to step right outside your door. Starting with a reasonable time goal (even just five minutes), head out for a walk around your neighborhood. Silence and tuck away your phone, then simply experience the nature around you. Even if it's winter, let yourself feel the chill on your face and breathe in the icy air. If it's hot and humid, feel the effect it has on your body. Where did you see or feel your Creator?

_____

_____

_____

_____

_____

_____

_____

_____

2

COME TO YOUR SENSES

GET OUTSIDE TODAY and see if you can engage all five senses. Some may be easier than others! Don't go inside until you've found a way to connect to each of the senses.

What sounds are you hearing?

_____

What does it smell like today?

_____

Is there anything you can taste when you breathe in?

_____

What sights draw your attention?

_____

What textures or sensations touch your head, brush your fingertips, lead your feet?

_____

3

TUNE IN TO PARKS AND RECREATION

Go online and research local parks, trails, and other outdoor spots in your area. Make a list of all the places you can find that are accessible to you. Include a few that seem outside the box or different from your normal places to go.

_____

_____

_____

_____

_____

_____

_____

_____

_____

_____

_____

_____

_____

_____

_____

_____

_____

_____

_____

_____

_____

Now, pick one place on the list that you can visit this week and put it on your schedule. See how many of the places on your list you can make it to this year.

4

LOOK FOR EACH
DAY OF CREATION

"For since the creation of the world God's invisible qualities—his eternal power and divine nature—have been clearly seen, being understood from what has been made, so that people are without excuse."

—Romans 1:20

THE APOSTLE PAUL EXPLAINS that God's qualities are revealed through the world He made. While He has revealed Himself in special ways, such as through the Word, God also reveals Himself generally through His creation. So careful attention and presence in natural settings can be a way to center ourselves in the Lord and worship Him.

One way to turn your attention to God is to use the outline of the creation story on pages 56–57. Meditate day by day and deliberately look for ways to experience those elements. In doing so, you can create a pattern of appreciating the different ways God has created this world and rest in the promise that He has made and is sovereign over it all. Take notes on what you feel is revealed.

DAY 1—God created light.

Feel the sun on your skin. Even if it's cloudy, look for the brightest spot you can find and notice how the light hits the clouds and trees and allows you to see.

_____

_____

DAY 2—God separated the waters and the sky.

Look at the skies and take in all of the colors you see. How many can you find? If you live near a river, lake, or ocean, venture out near the shores and touch the water. Allow it to point to the greatness of the Creator.

_____

_____

DAY 3—God created the dry land and filled it with plants.

Walk outside onto the grass, maybe even take your shoes off! Feel as much vegetation as you can, from the leaves and bark on the trees to the blades of grass.

_____

_____

DAY 4—God created the sun, moon, stars, and planets.
Go outside at night and look at the moon and stars. There may even be other planets visible. What's the brightest star you see? Consider what it's like to worship a God who has created the entirety of the universe.

_____

_____

DAY 5—God created the birds and sea creatures.
Be a bird watcher for a day! See how many different birds you can find outside. Listen for the calls they make and marvel at the diversity in just this one species of animal.

_____

_____

DAY 6—God created humans and land animals.
Take a look at your fellow humans. Say hello or check in with someone today. Look for animals outside and point them out to other people around you. See if you can share a little moment of wonder with another person.

_____

_____

Boundaries help us to distinguish our property so that we can take care of it.
—HENRY CLOUD

TRUST THE RAILINGS

WHAT DO YOU THINK OF when you think of boundaries? Do you think of walls, restrictions, limitations? Or do you think of freedom, protection, and peace?

Imagine this scenario: You're crossing a bridge without railings. On either side of your path, you look down a hundred feet to the cold water below. How anxiety-provoking would that be? Now, imagine there are secure railings attached to each side. You're still a hundred feet high, but the railings (or boundaries) provide walking safety. In which scenario would you feel more comfortable?

Healthy boundaries help create a safe, enjoyable, and sustainable lifestyle. They protect us from burnout and exhaustion as we wisely steward our time, energy, and attention. They help us take responsibility for what truly belongs to us, respect what belongs to other people, and prevent us from practicing our own or enabling others' codependent behavior. By learning when to say yes and when to say no, we mitigate frustration, resentment, irritability, and anger.

This unit will help you see how boundaries protect our internal and external resources to promote health and growth. Without such boundaries, we risk exposing ourselves to harmful or chronically chaotic people, situations, and habits that will increase our anxiety.

1

TAKE A BOUNDARIES INVENTORY

Proverbs 2:3 instructs us to "call out for insight and cry aloud for understanding." What barriers do you need to set in place with those who are abusive, harmful, or draining to you? Are there areas where your boundaries are too rigid and leave you isolated from God and others?

AS YOU GO ABOUT YOUR DAY, discern what boundaries you may need to implement, adjust, or remove. Don't wait until the end of the day to assess; jot down thoughts on paper or in an app as soon as they come to you. Then collate the insights here later.

Implement

_____

_____

_____

_____

Adjust

_____

_____

_____

_____

Remove

_____

_____

_____

_____

2

START WITH A SMALL NO

IF YOU'RE NERVOUS OR ANXIOUS to start setting a boundary, practice saying no or "that won't work for me." List three small ways and one larger situation in which you can say no this week to say yes to healthy boundaries.

1. _____

_____

2. _____

_____

3. _____

_____

4. _____

_____

HOW DOES IT FEEL when your boundaries are/aren't respected? How does this affect the rest of your day and interactions with others?

_____

_____

_____

_____

_____

_____

_____

_____

_____

_____

_____

_____

_____

3

GET OTHERS ON BOARD

Boundaries are most effective when they are communicated clearly. Perhaps you'll start with people who noticeably practice their own healthy boundary-setting and will respect yours. People like this will honor your efforts to budget and protect your internal resources. Then, when you've built up your strength, consider ways to establish boundaries with people who are dismissive or disrespectful of them. Just like anything else, this will take practice.

MAKE A LIST OF PEOPLE to share boundaries with, jot down notes about how, when, and where to approach them with the discussion.

1. _____

_____

2. _____

_____

3. _____

_____

4. _____

_____

5. _____

_____

SET PHYSICAL BOUNDARIES

IF YOU HAVE TROUBLE KEEPING ONE AREA of life separate from another, consider using a physical boundary as a mental boundary. For example, if you're constantly thinking about work at home, make your car a work boundary. You can think about work while in your car, but once you leave and enter your home, no thinking about work is allowed. Linking a physical boundary to a mental boundary takes practice but is a helpful exercise in keeping life's stressors and anxieties in their place. What physical boundaries could help you?

_____

_____

_____

_____

_____

_____

_____

5

AUDIT YOURSELF

SOMETIMES THE BOUNDARIES THAT WORKED for us at one point now prevent us from enjoying a fuller life. Life and relationships are not static. Take time at a yearly milestone (maybe your birthday or January 1) to think about the boundaries in your life. Do they need an adjustment or tearing down, or do new ones need to be built? Ask God to help you throughout this process and give you the grace to use boundaries for safety, protection, edification, and connection.

My prayer for wise boundaries:

_____

_____

_____

_____

_____

_____

_____

_____

Blessed are the flexible, for they shall not be broken.

—MODERN-DAY PROVERB

FLEX INTO BLESSINGS

LIFE THROWS US CURVEBALLS. It could be as little as realizing that a favorite coffee shop is closed for the day, or as big as the sudden death of a loved one. The former is easier to adjust to; the latter, not so much. The point here is that we cannot control everything in our lives. Most people know this on an intellectual level, but when the chaos gets real and our day goes sideways, many hold rigid and snap rather than bend and adjust to what life gives them.

Anxiety makes us want to escape, run, clam up, or shut down, all of which are tendencies to protect against immediate danger—and that makes sense! However, while protective, they don't always serve to help us deal with anxiety effectively. Instead, we need resilience. Resilience is the ability to bend, not break, bounce back, and perhaps even grow. Being resilient does not mean a person will never experience anxiety; it's a way through the storms we all inevitably face.

One way we become resilient, strangely enough, is not by fighting against life but by accepting the reality that it gives us. We will always have the conflict between how we want life to go and how it actually plays out, but we can learn to be more comfortable sacrificing what we want (or think we want) in order to accept whatever it is that comes to us. On the far end of this, we may even find ourselves experiencing joy in life as we loosen our grip on control. Let the exercises in this unit guide you toward that goal.

1

STRETCH YOURSELF

IN THE SPIRIT OF FLEXIBILITY, try literally becoming more flexible. Find five gentle stretches to incorporate into your day. These are best done after a short workout (light walking, weight lifting, jogging, or biking) when your body has warmed up.

How do you feel before you stretch versus how you feel after?

_____

_____

_____

How can you remind yourself of this feeling as you aim for more flexibility in other areas of your life? (Example: Post words or pictures—on your mirror or in your daily planner—that capture the feeling of sinking into surrender of all that tightness.)

_____

_____

_____

2

REFLECT ON A CURVEBALL

IF YOU'VE EVER WATCHED BASEBALL, you've seen a player watch the film of an at bat afterward in the dugout. They are looking for lessons learned—how they handled that curveball. You can go back to your day or week in the same way. Get curious about a curveball you experienced, being careful to look for God's wisdom and not linger in regret.

What happened today or this week that did not go as you wanted or expected it to?

_____

How did you react? What did you feel when things shifted?

_____

How could you have been more flexible in the moment? Would you have felt better then and now?

_____

_____

_____

3

KNOW YOUR NORTH STAR

FEELINGS OF ANXIETY often flow out of a fear of abandonment. We worry that we will be left on our own. While we can't always control who comes and goes in our lives, we can rely on one constant strengthening presence. Read John 10:27–30:

"My sheep listen to my voice; I know them, and they follow me. I give them eternal life, and they shall never perish; no one will snatch them out of my hand. My Father, who has given them to me, is greater than all; no one can snatch them out of my Father's hand. I and the Father are one."

Read those words of reassurance from Jesus two more times slowly.

How do His words speak to your fears?

_____

_____

How can you remind yourself that no matter what happens you can look to Jesus?

_____

_____

4

TAKE OUT THE TRASH

WHENEVER YOU FIND that you're having a hard time with release, write a few words to sum up the situation on a piece of paper. Pray and ask God that, as you throw the paper in the trash (or the shredder), He would give you the peace to truly let go. Is there something in your life right now that needs to get buried in the trash ASAP?

_____

_____

_____

_____

_____

_____

_____

_____

Give me Your eyes
for just one second.
Give me Your eyes so
I can see everything
that I keep missing.
—BRANDON HEATH

BORROW GOD'S EYES

HOW DO YOU SEE YOURSELF? Most people see themselves through their own imperfect eyes or the eyes of others—friends, enemies, parents, bosses, even social media followers. When your view of yourself is based solely on those human sources and society's ever-changing standards, it can lead to feelings of unworthiness. You risk becoming restless, discontent, hopeless, confused, and anxious.

But we can go to God for the real story—the true story He holds out to us, longing for us to accept. Regardless of what you see when you look in the mirror, God sees the you He has created, chosen, and called. In the belly of the whale, God sees you as a great prophet. As a young shepherd boy forgotten by his family, God sees you as an anointed king after His own heart. As the scandalized woman who endures the scorching midday sun to retrieve water from the well, God sees you as worthy and a marvelous evangelist. When you see yourself as feeble, God sees you as a mighty warrior leading a small army to great victory.

Rest assured that how God sees you in your darkest moments is far gentler and more compassionate than your view of yourself. Always remember: You were God's decision. His powerful Spirit is in you. His loving eyes are on you. The exercises in this unit will lead you to bind these truths to your heart.

1

SPEAK TO YOURSELF WITH LOVE

You are the temple of the Holy Spirit. You are where God chooses to dwell. Because of Christ, God has chosen to abide in His people. Consider what negative thoughts tend to pop up when you look in the mirror. How can you replace those thoughts with gratitude and affirm the truth that you are the dwelling place of God?

My judgment	Replaced with praise

EXAMPLES:

I wish I didn't have so many wrinkles.	I'm grateful for the laugh lines (and even worry lines) that remind me of the full life God has given me.
I hate the shape of my body.	Thank you, Lord, for designing the life-sustaining functions of my body.

Are there other ways you could be more caring and compassionate toward your body, the place where the Lord has chosen to abide?

TAKE A SOCIAL MEDIA BREAK

Fasting allows you to abstain from one thing to fill yourself with something better. To set yourself up for success, plan how long you'll fast from social media and prepare what you will do instead. Schedule times to get together with God and people whom you are able to connect with emotionally. Plan activities that you once delighted in.

AS YOU CARRY OUT YOUR PLAN, notice and record your thoughts, feelings, and bodily sensations. What was different? How do you need to engage with social media in a healthier way?

_____

_____

_____

_____

_____

_____

_____

_____

When you go back to your social media consumption, continue to notice and honestly record your feelings, thoughts, sensations, and moods in a journal.

FIND A LOVING LENS

TURN TO YOUR BIBLE WITH CURIOSITY about how God sees His children. Write the Scripture verses you find that speak to you below.

_____

_____

_____

_____

_____

_____

_____

_____

_____

Choose one verse or phrase and put it on an index card to keep with you, or take a photo and use it as your phone's wallpaper.

EXTEND THE LENS

TAKE YOUR LIST FROM "Find a Loving Lens" on page 80 and commit to meditating on one verse on the list each month. As you read Scripture and see more of how God sees His children, you can add to your list. Finally, don't keep the list to yourself. What are some ways you can share a loving lens with others?

We have this hope as an anchor for the soul, firm and secure.

—HEBREWS 6:19A

ANCHOR YOUR HOPE

THERE'S SOMETHING COMFORTING about watching a TV series or movie we've seen before. It's a familiar story that brings up good feelings. We know the characters, we know the storyline, and, best of all, we know how it ends. As believers in Christ, we know how our story ends too. The Book of Revelation tells us about Christ's ultimate and complete victory over sin and death and describes the new heaven and earth that will be our home with God for the rest of eternity.

When you become a believer, nowhere in the Word does God promise your life will get easier. Jesus even acknowledges that suffering is inevitable on this side of heaven, but in John 16:33 He also reminds us of the hope we have: "I have told you these things, so that in me you may have peace. In this world you will have trouble. But take heart! I have overcome the world." Leading up to this verse, Jesus was preparing the disciples for His imminent suffering, death, and departure. He tells them they will weep and mourn and grieve, but after a while, their grief will turn to joy that cannot be taken away.

In the same way, we can also have joy because of whom we place our hope in. The disciples didn't know what was coming, but we do. We have God's Word as the assurance of our salvation. Our hope steadies us and keeps us secure even in great suffering, loss, and chaos. Let's remind ourselves of that anchor with every exercise in this section.

CHECK YOUR SOURCE

IN ENGLAND THEY HAVE A PHRASE, "It's the hope that kills you." To protect against disappointment, it seems better to set expectations low.

Write about a time when your hopes were dashed. What did hope look like going into the situation? What was your source of hope? How did the loss of that hope impact you? How did it affect your relationship with God?

_____

_____

_____

_____

_____

_____

_____

_____

_____

_____

KNOW THE HOPE
THAT HOLDS UP

WRITE ABOUT A TIME WHEN YOU HAD HOPE during a dark season. How was this experience different from the situation you wrote about in "Check Your Source" on page 84? Consider: What did hope look like? How did your hope encourage you? What was your source of hope?

_____

_____

_____

_____

_____

_____

_____

_____

_____

_____

_____

3

CONSIDER THE CIRCUMSTANCES

I have learned the secret of being content in any and every situation, whether well fed or hungry, whether living in plenty or in want. I can do all this through him who gives me strength.

—Philippians 4:12b–13

A NEW PRESIDENT? A BETTER JOB? In what or whom do we place our hopes? The answer to this question reveals things about ourselves as well as what we desire in life. In what or whom are you placing your hope right now? What do you think will happen in your life if those hopes become realized? Are your hopes realistic and able to bring lasting peace?

CREATE YOUR HOPE IMAGE

Read the account of the new heaven and new earth in Revelation 21:1–4. Then, in the space that follows or on a separate paper, draw, color, or paint a picture of what you imagine God's Kingdom will be like based on this passage. Title your artwork with your favorite verse about hope, such as Romans 15:13: "May the God of hope fill you with all joy and peace as you trust in him, so that you may overflow with hope by the power of the Holy Spirit." Consider placing your hope image in a place where you will see it every day, or place a bookmark in this page to bring you back when you need a hope reminder.

We must not allow
other people's limited
perceptions to define us.
—VIRGINIA SATIR

BOUNCE BACK
FROM REJECTION

~~~~~~~~~~

REJECTION HURTS—there's no way around it. We've all experienced it at some point. Applying for a job, asking someone out on a date, speaking in public—these are just a few things that stir up fears of being ridiculed, turned down, or ignored. Lots of anxious people hold a core memory of a time when they felt crushed by rejection. Another person's words or actions made them feel unworthy of affection, friendship, or time. It might have hurt so bad that they vowed never to let it happen again and go to great lengths to avoid any risk of rejection.

Did you know Jesus was rejected many times? It's wild to think about God in the flesh being rejected by sinful humanity. When Jesus returned to His hometown and preached in the synagogue, many people took offense. They said things like, "Isn't this that carpenter? Mary's son?" They thought He was some ordinary guy with no authority to speak such wisdom. Jesus was the "stone the builders rejected that had become the cornerstone."

So, how did Jesus handle rejection? He acknowledged it and then continued on His mission. He did not let it stop Him from going to the next town and ministering to new people—whom He gave the freedom to accept or reject Him as well. Ultimately, Jesus remained focused on His purpose. And there's a lot to learn in that: the truth is that rejection doesn't define us, and neither do the people who reject us, as the exercises in this unit will help you see.

1

LOOK BACK WITH JESUS

On a good day, what beliefs do you have about your
abilities, character, and worth?

_____

_____

_____

Think about a time you've experienced rejection. How did
you feel about yourself? About the person who rejected you?

_____

_____

_____

Thinking about how Jesus faced rejection, how do you now
feel about that situation?

_____

_____

_____

FACE YOUR FEARS

LIST SOME FEARS YOU HAVE about getting rejected. For example, "I'm afraid I'm going to bomb this job interview, I won't get the job, and my family will be disappointed in me." Then write down what you would do next if that were to happen.

Fear	Reaction
_____	_____
_____	_____
_____	_____
_____	_____
_____	_____

In what ways are your reactions similar to those of Jesus? In what ways are they not?

3

CARRY THE TRUTH

HOW CAN YOU COUNTER someone's rejection of you with what God says about you? Ponder some of these verses:

- **ROMANS 8:28**
  "And we know that in all things God works for the good of those who love him, who have been called according to his purpose."

- **GALATIANS 1:10**
  "Am I now trying to win the approval of human beings, or of God? Or am I trying to please people? If I were still trying to please people, I would not be a servant of Christ."

- **JOHN 15:18**
  "If the world hates you, keep in mind that it hated me first."

- **PSALM 139:14A**
  "I praise you because I am fearfully and wonderfully made."

- **ROMANS 8:1**
  "There is now no condemnation for those who are in Christ Jesus."

CHOOSE A VERSE that God is leading you to apply to your fears or doubts. Write it out in bold lettering below, then letter it on a sticky note or an index card and place it somewhere you'll see often. Better yet, commit this verse to memory so you can have it on your heart and mind when you're going into a situation with the risk of rejection. Remind yourself that the God who created you knows you and loves you more than anyone else in this world. He has the final say about who you are.

We are usually surrounded by so much outer noise that it is hard to truly hear our God when he is speaking to us.

—HENRI NOUWEN

STILL THE NOISE

~~~~~~

THROUGHOUT THE GOSPELS, Jesus models the importance of solitude. Jesus repeatedly goes to a solitary place to commune with and rest in the Father. He knew that power, direction, clarity, and energy come from our "being" in the Father. This, in turn, gives our "doing" purpose and efficacy.

We live in a world that praises independence, ambition, and self-seeking. When asked how they are doing, many say with pride that they're "busy," not realizing that busyness without purpose, boundaries, and quiet hinders abundant life. The busier you are, the more necessary solitude is.

What's the difference between isolation and solitude? Isolation is avoidance and withdrawal, a loss of connection from yourself and others, including God. Solitude, on the other hand, is carving out time to be alone for the purpose of grounding in, filling from, and connecting with God. Solitude centers you in the truth that we are in the care of a loving Father who knows each star by name. No detail is too small for His love. No great matter can overwhelm Him. In solitude, we remember that He is in control and we are not expected to do His job.

In the intentional stillness and quietness of solitude, we learn that although we are spending time alone, we are not lonely. We realize the deep blessing of eternal companionship with the Holy Spirit, our advocate, comforter, and guide who leads us in truth. Let's enter into that kind of time in this unit.

1

WRITE OUT YOUR FLEETING FEELINGS

Sometimes, we avoid being alone because we fear being overcome by anxiety and feeling overwhelmed. Try spending even just a few minutes in complete solitude today with only the company of a writing utensil and this workbook. You'll start to learn that feelings are fleeting and that you have a great capacity to endure discomfort. A practice of welcoming discomfort in God's presence will expand your window of tolerance to the stress and distress of day-to-day life.

If things start to feel overwhelming or your anxiety rises, write it out in the space below.

_____

_____

_____

_____

_____

_____

_____

_____

_____

_____

_____

_____

_____

_____

_____

2

TAKE A MINI RETREAT

For a set amount of time, choose to retreat to a pleasant place. Maybe you start with just ten to twenty minutes first thing in the morning. Wherever you go, embrace what the present moment offers. Take care to not look at your phone, read text messages, or check email until after your retreat is done. Don't talk, don't plan out your day, don't listen to a podcast. Just *be* and experience what is around you.

At some point later in the day, sketch or describe what it felt like to take this set-apart time.

TRY AN INTENTIONAL TO-DO

SCHEDULE INTO YOUR DAY some self-care to rest and relax in the Lord. Maybe that looks like taking a power nap, soaking in a warm bath, or performing progressive muscle relaxation, meditation, or visualization exercises using the truth of Scripture to offer groundedness and renewal. There are lots of Christian meditation apps and YouTube channels that use prayer and Scripture to speak truth into your heart as you take your daily time. Come back later and record what you chose to do and how it affected your day.

4

FIND STRENGTH
IN THE QUIET

NOW THAT YOU'VE EXPERIENCED THE POWER of
spending time in stillness, try introducing daily quiet time—a discipline
of setting aside time to delight in the Lord through Scripture and
prayer. Quiet time could be most effective in the morning, before
others in your household wake up and before your daily duties begin.
What could work best for you?

_____

How can your quiet time help you use your spiritual gifts? What can
you receive from the Lord in the morning that you can share with
others throughout the day—a verse, word of counsel, encouragement,
insight, or affectionate gratitude?

_____

_____

_____

_____

Rather than living
every day as if it's
my *last*, I've shifted to a
gentler approach of living
every day as if it's my *first*.
—SULEIKA JAOUAD

FIND CALM IN CURIOSITY

OUR GOD WELCOMES OUR QUESTIONS and embraces our curiosity. Just look to the Bible to see Habakkuk, David, Job, Mary, Joseph, Moses, Zacchaeus, Nicodemus, the disciples, the woman at the well . . . and the list could go on. Jesus—the discerner of our hearts, minds, and intents—also approached people with curiosity. From childhood to the Ascension, Christ asked questions that drew His listeners to the deep well of God's wisdom. His questions—from "Did you not know that I must be about My Father's business?" to "Peter, do you love me?"—directed the listener to dive beneath the surface and rise up with more clarity about God and oneself.

Curiosity is an openness to set aside assumptions and expand our understanding. To be curious is to assume the position of a child—eager to learn, know, and understand. God has never rebuked a curious person; instead, an eager person who brings their fear, doubt, or broken heart to the Lord will be satisfied, sometimes with answers and always with knowing the Lord's heart more deeply and intimately.

Curiosity also has a way of slowing us down, pulling us deep, and guiding us without fear. Life becomes more interesting, and the humanity of others becomes more palpable as we shift the focus from us to them. Suddenly, we are freed from having to be right and from the fear of being wrong. Curiosity ushers anxiety aside and says, "Rest here awhile. There might be something for you to learn." The exercises in this unit guide you into curiosity and the calm it can offer.

1

EXPLORE NEW TASTES

HIT A LOCAL RESTAURANT THAT OFFERS ETHNIC FOOD, visit a cultural festival, or try a new recipe from a culture unfamiliar to you. Engage in a conversation with the waiter, chef, or friend about the food and learn the history of or a fun fact about what you are eating. As you eat, be curious and mindful in the moment. What flavors, textures, and aromas come through?

_____

_____

_____

What factors or assumptions may have held you back from enjoying this food before? How did it feel to set all that aside and try something new?

_____

_____

_____

2

GET INSPIRED BY A CHILD

CURIOSITY HAS A CHILDLIKE ELEMENT TO IT. Watch a young child in your life as they curiously explore something new, interesting, or unknown. Notice their facial expressions, body language, tone of voice, inflections, and movement. What strikes you?

_____

_____

_____

_____

_____

_____

_____

_____

Whenever you start to notice your own rigidity and resistance in new situations, recall a child's curious reaction to guide you into a calmer, more joyful experience.

3

INVITE EMOTIONS
FOR A VISIT

WHAT EMOTIONS ARE YOU HONESTLY FEELING right now?
List them in the left column.

Feeling	Message
_____	_____
_____	_____
_____	_____
_____	_____
_____	_____

Now go back and, without judging the emotion as good or bad, simply think about what the emotion could be trying to tell you.

To keep this practice going on a regular basis, create a guestbook where you can write down the messages received from various emotions. Invite every emotion to come in as a guest, not a resident, to deliver wisdom. Emotions can stay for a limited time and must adhere to boundaries set by you, the owner of the house. Receive the message from the emotion and then release it.

4

QUEST TO BE A GOOD QUESTIONER

PRACTICE USING OPEN-ENDED QUESTIONS in conversation—questions that cannot be answered with yes or no and that require more explanation. Seek to connect rather than correct, especially if you're in a position of leadership. Give time for others to think about and formulate their response, and actively listen to them. What happens when you try these steps?

_____

_____

_____

Don't assume you can't practice curiosity with the people you know most intimately. We are always changing, growing, discovering, struggling, wrestling, and overcoming. Each person can teach you at least one new thing despite how young, old, or different they are. What surprising new teachings have you received from people close to you?

_____

_____

_____

When we focus on ourselves, our world contracts as our problems and preoccupations loom large. But when we focus on others, our world expands.

—DANIEL GOLEMAN

FOCUS OUTWARD

~~~~~~

MORE AND MORE, people are living with very little "bandwidth" in their lives. Ironically, this lack of bandwidth is influenced by our constant connection to technology, which, among other things, increases work hours.

The costs of not having bandwidth or of being busy are many. We often think of the obvious cost, which is a lack of physical energy. However, the emotional and spiritual costs can be even more pronounced. Loss of empathy is one of the costliest aspects of individual and societal busyness. As we become busier, we also become more self-focused, a natural offshoot of all our responsibilities. Even if some of these responsibilities came originally from a place of empathy, we can lose our empathy in the process. This increase in focus on the self can greatly decrease our empathy with others. In addition, this imbalance of self-focus exacerbates anxiety.

This phenomenon exists in individuals, families, and churches and throughout society. It begs the question, why do we constantly "eat the apple" and think we know more about how to live than God? God finds joy in true connection and relationship, as did Jesus in His time on earth. They both knew when to rest and just *be*, alone and in the presence of others. Why do we think we don't need to? This section will help you see the power of a pause for connection.

1

SEE WHO JESUS SENDS

"So from now on we regard no one from a worldly point of view. Though we once regarded Christ in this way, we do so no longer."

—2 Corinthians 5:16

BECAUSE OF CHRIST, WE VIEW EVERYONE we meet as eternal beings who have an eternal destiny. How can this truth impact our lives? If humility is connected to movement away from anxiety, we grow in humility not by trying to be humble. We grow in humility and away from pride by thinking of and deliberately caring for others.

We are so often consumed with our lives and daily worries that we fail to notice those around us. Who are the people you encounter as you go through any ordinary day? Write down as many names as you can remember from your comings and goings today or yesterday.

_____

_____

_____

_____

_____

_____

_____

Try doing this exercise again a week from now. With new intention, you will likely remember more people.

PRAY FOR THOSE
ON YOUR PATH

TAKE THE LIST FROM THE FIRST EXERCISE and, before
you start your day, pray for opportunities to connect in some way
with the people whose names you've written. Come back later and
record your experiences.

_____

_____

_____

_____

_____

_____

_____

_____

3

PLAN FOR CONNECTIONS

NOW, IT'S TIME TO TAKE YOUR CONNECTIONS a step further. How can you plan during your day to connect more deeply with the people you encounter regularly?

_____

_____

_____

_____

_____

_____

_____

_____

You will likely become better at showing empathy and loving people well and see a reduction in your own level of anxiety as you focus a little less on yourself.

She gave this name
to the LORD who spoke
to her: "You are the God
who sees me," for she said,
"I have now seen the
One who sees me."

—GENESIS 16:13

SEE GOD SEEING YOU

MANY OF US HAVE AN INTERNALIZED PICTURE of ·
God tapping His foot, looking at His watch, impatiently waiting for us
to get our act together. It's like we hear Him saying, "Would you just
trust me for once?"

Thankfully, how we believe God feels about us when we experience
anxiety doesn't dictate how He actually feels. God speaks for Himself!
When He says that He feels a certain way about us, we don't have
the power to change that. In our soul, we can see God seeing us with
compassion—not as weak or a burden or a failure. More than just
knowing, we can experience the tenderness in His gaze on us.

So, how does God see us if not with indignation, impatience, or
disappointment? Jesus says, "As the Father has loved me, so have
I loved you. Now remain in my love" (John 15:9). God loves us with
the same intensity and depth of love that exists between Him and
Jesus. This is unrelenting, unblemished, unadulterated love. This is not
diminished when we can't conjure up the strength or willpower to find
victory over our anxiety, even if we are disappointed with ourselves.
When we experience anxiety and feel embarrassed for being at a loss,
that is the very moment when we can embrace and rest in God's love
for us that is always complete. Practice entering into that assurance
with the exercises in this unit.

BE STILL AND KNOW

GO TO A PLACE WHERE YOU FEEL AT REST—maybe
outdoors in nature or sitting with a cup of coffee near a window where
the sun is streaming in. Let your mind and body still as you focus on
how God cares for you. Try to tune in to the love that surrounds you.
Then, after a few minutes, write whatever prayer comes to you to ask
that the Lord, through His Spirit, would bring you to know and believe
in your heart how He sees you in your anxiety.

_____

_____

_____

_____

_____

_____

_____

RECOGNIZE THE POWER OF LOVE

THINK OF SOMEONE WHO HAS CARED FOR YOU when you were feeling anxious. What words did they say that brought comfort and assured you of your relationship with them? Recall the power of their love and lift up thanks to God for putting that person in your life. If you can't think of anyone, what do you wish someone would say to you when you're feeling anxious? Pray that someone would come into your life with that love you need.

_____

_____

_____

_____

_____

_____

_____

3

LOOK UPON HIS FACE

WITH YOUR EYES CLOSED, SIT SILENTLY and picture God looking at you. What's the expression on His face? Sketch or write about it in the space that follows.

Remember that, in reality, He looks at you with unconditional love. If you didn't see positive expressions the first time, close your eyes again and see if you can imagine that look of loving understanding on His face, and have faith that it's true. If you continue to see anything other than loving understanding, ask yourself who in your life has looked at you with the face you've seen. Remind yourself that God isn't in that. As you wrestle with different difficulties throughout your life, remember and call to mind God's true, loving gaze.

4

MATCH EMOTION TO PROVISION

TO HELP YOU RECALL THE COMPLETENESS OF GOD and His love for you, find different names or characteristics given to God within Scripture. List them below along with the feelings they could help you through. Example: When you feel fearful or lost, you may call out to God as your "strong tower" (Psalm 61:3) or "my fortress and my deliverer" (Psalm 18:2).

Name of God	Feelings

In their hearts
humans plan their
course, but the LORD
establishes their steps.
—PROVERBS 16:9

SURRENDER
YOUR STEPS

IF YOU'VE EVER PLAYED WITH A CHINESE FINGER TRAP, you probably ended up with your fingers stuck. The harder you pull to free yourself, the tighter it squeezes your fingers inside it. Paradoxically, the way to get unstuck is to push your fingers toward the center and release your natural instinct to pull with your own strength.

The first strategy is also how many of us approach life, giving in to the natural human desire to grab power over our lives. We want the freedom to decide how we spend our time, where we live, what we consume, and how we fulfill our needs, to name a few. But the more we fight to maintain control, our fingers get further caught in the trap. We can get so far into reliance on ourselves. That is, until something unexpected happens that quickly reminds us of how little control we actually have—a natural disaster, a grim diagnosis, or a car accident. We've been kidding ourselves all along.

The stories of Jacob and Jonah show us that fighting against God's will never ends well. Sure, they had the free will to do so, but in the end, they just exhausted themselves and caused unnecessary heartache. This is similar to what happens when we attempt to exert control over the big and little things to ensure they go our way. The exercises in this unit will help you remember that surrendering is the path to peace and freedom.

1

SEE THE BETTER PLANS

We were gifted with free will. At the same time, we were designed to be completely dependent on God. Throughout the Word, we're reminded of this. During His Sermon on the Mount, Jesus tells the crowd not to worry about their lives, or what they will eat or wear. He tells them to look at the birds. They don't sow, reap, or store food. God still provides for them. The flowers, trees, and grass of the fields all grow, bloom, and are nourished season after season. God has this whole world under control. This includes each and every one of us as well.

TO SURRENDER REQUIRES ABSOLUTE TRUST that God will provide you with everything you need. Jesus sums this up at the end of Matthew 6 in verse 33: "Seek first his kingdom and his righteousness, and all these things will be given to you as well." Surrender means placing God and His Word in the place of ultimate authority over every part of your life. It means seeking Him in every decision and trusting that He has better plans for you than you could ever have for yourself. It's believing that God sees eternity from start to finish and has you exactly where He intends for you to be.

What are some things you fear losing control over?

_____

_____

_____

What do you fear will happen if you surrender these things to God?

_____

_____

What has been the cost of holding on to them?

_____

_____

2

FEEL THE WEIGHT

Fill a backpack or bag with ten to twenty pounds of books, then walk around with it for a time and feel the weight. The physical weight of the bag pales in comparison to what you are carrying emotionally. You can put the bag down and detach yourself from the burden. But when you can't seem to surrender control to God, your worries are always with you, weighing you down.

THE FIRST STEP IN CHANGE is often deeper insight. How do you feel walking with the physical and emotional weight? Are you ready to surrender and find release (even joy!)?

As you empty the bag of books, read out loud your list of fears from exercise 1. When the bag is empty, lift it up as you recite 1 Peter 5:6–7: "Humble yourselves, therefore, under God's mighty hand, that he may lift you up in due time. Cast all your anxiety on him because he cares for you."

This is the promise that God has for you. Remember, God is not angry with you because you struggle to let go. He just doesn't want to see you weighed down.

GO BOLDLY TO JESUS

SURRENDER ISN'T LIKELY TO COME OVERNIGHT.
But each step will move you closer to God and away from unnecessary worry. To help you discern some first steps, meditate on Jesus's words to Bartimaeus in Mark 10:51: "What do you want me to do for you?"

Bartimaeus, unlike the others in the crowd, had a very personal interaction with Jesus. Why? He called out to Jesus. He basically said, "Jesus, pay some attention to me!" Jesus did. He was bold even in the face of ridicule. That was how much he wanted to be healed.

If you were to boldly go to Jesus, what would you ask for Him to do to help you release control and take steps toward surrender? Gather your needs here and then take them to Him.

MARK THE MILESTONES

WHEN YOU BECOME A CHRISTIAN, you give what you know of yourself to what you know of God. As you grow, God reveals new things about Himself to you and He also reveals truths about you. You see, our relationship with God is one of *continual* surrender. Each year, write down the things that you have learned about God as well as what has been revealed about you. If you want, you can write it on a wall like your parents did when they recorded your height on your birthday! Wherever you keep a record, make sure it's somewhere you can see it regularly. What could you mark as milestones from the past year?

_____

_____

_____

_____

_____

_____

_____

"Come to me,
all you who are weary
and burdened, and
I will give you rest."
—MATTHEW 11:28

REST IN HIS CARE

~~~~~~~

SLEEP IS OFTEN ONE OF THE FIRST THINGS impacted by anxiety. You may lie awake, thoughts racing as you struggle to slow down and find quiet. The minutes tick by, and the anxiety heightens as you glance at the clock and try to calculate how much sleep you could still get if only you could fall asleep *right now*. In the morning, you attempt to salvage as much energy as you can, looking to the night ahead with both dread and hope that maybe you'll find rest.

Sleeplessness and sleep disruption are common symptoms of anxiety. Yet, sleep is also one of the primary defenses the Lord has given us against anxiety. It is a precious commodity. A sleepless night will have an almost immediate impact on the body and the mind. Concentration goes down, emotions are less stable, and the ability to manage stress is diminished. In the same way, getting just one good night of sleep can directly address each of these effects and start you on a path toward a better day.

To manage anxious thoughts, you need to improve your sleep habits. Thankfully, there are some easy steps you could start taking today to build up a healthier sleep routine over time.

1

DROP YOUR WORRIES

In the evening, find a quiet and peaceful place
other than your bedroom to stop and get all
the cares of the day out of your head and onto
paper. (Your bedroom needs to stay associated
with rest and sleep.) Often, writing things
down, in and of itself, will help us to put worries
in perspective and give us some distance from
them before sleep.

Take time with this and make it an exhaustive list.

_____

_____

_____

_____

_____

_____

_____

_____

_____

_____

_____

_____

_____

_____

_____

2

TURN TO A VERSE

"He will not let your foot slip—he who watches over you will not slumber; indeed, he who watches over Israel will neither slumber nor sleep."

—Psalm 121:3–4

ON THOSE NIGHTS WHEN YOU FIND YOURSELF
tossing and turning, thoughts spiraling in all directions, find your
center. Think of a short verse (like the one on the previous page) or
a prayer you can easily remember. Slow your breathing, center your
heart on the Lord, and pray or recite those words in your mind slowly
and on repeat. As you do this, allow the words to permeate your being
and remind you of the Lord's faithfulness.

**Find and write out some verses that bring you calm and
comfort for the next time you can't sleep.**

DESIGN A SLEEP ROUTINE

CONSIDER HOW YOU SPEND THE EVENING hours leading up to bedtime. What can you slot in and out that may support better sleep? Examples:

+ I will go screen-free after ＿＿ p.m. and put my phone on "do not disturb" except for emergency contacts from ＿＿ p.m. to ＿＿ a.m.

+ The snack cabinet closes by ＿＿ p.m.

+ I'll make sure to turn the thermostat down to ＿＿ by ＿＿ p.m.

_____

_____

_____

_____

_____

_____

LEARN YOUR SLEEP STYLE

CREATING NEW SLEEP HABITS starts with understanding your current habits. Take an honest look at yourself as you consider:

+ Do you feel more rested when you go to bed at 9:00 or 11:00 (or another time)?

+ What thoughts tend to keep you up at night? How are you addressing your anxious thoughts when you're awake?

+ What boundaries might help protect your sleep?

Use a journal or sleep-tracking app to help see areas you need to pray over or ask for help. What insights emerge? What provisions does God want to offer for better sleep? What blessings could come as an outcome of better sleep?

_____

_____

_____

_____

If you look for perfection, you'll never be content.

—LEO TOLSTOY

REMEMBER WHOSE YOU ARE

SOMETIMES ANXIETY CAN BE ROOTED in an inaccurate picture of ourselves. Thinking too optimistically about ourselves can make us self-righteous and lead us to think we are better than others. We can put a lot of pressure on ourselves to live up to some perfect image. On the other hand, when we are abrasively pessimistic, we refuse to see the talents that God gave us. This leads to being easily shamed and more prone to negative self-talk.

You might not realize it, but thinking patterns affect our relationships with others as well. How you see yourself has a huge impact on how you think others see you! Listen to too much negative self-talk, and you will begin to think that eyes are always on you, and you will not be confident in who you are for fear of being criticized.

Gideon was from the weakest clan in Manasseh and the least among his family. Considering his circumstances, he had every right to doubt his abilities. Instead, he relied on what God called him: "mighty warrior." In holding to what God said about him, he already knew he had what it took to rescue his people from their enemy. Gideon could have stayed in the fear of the unknown, but he decided to act out his faith in trusting God's promises despite not knowing exactly what it would look like. We too can ease our anxieties by trusting in God's promises and listening to what He tells us about ourselves.

1

AIM FOR BEAUTIFUL, NOT PERFECT

JESUS DID NOT GO TO THE CROSS FOR US TO TRY to earn our salvation through the burden of perfectionism. If you are alive "in Christ," you are made, declared, and surely seen as perfect in the eyes of the One who matters—God.

What parts of your day are you still thinking about and wish you had done more to measure up in worldly terms? List them in the first column.

_____   _____

_____   _____

_____   _____

_____   _____

_____   _____

Now go back and write "good enough!" next to each entry. Then write "God loves good enough!" on a sticky note and post it somewhere you will see it every morning.

CONSIDER WHAT JESUS WANTS

IT IS HARD TO LET GO OF THINGS that have our hearts. But when we seek Jesus first, we are able to loosen our grip on money, relationships, and expectations. Reflect on an area of your life you have not fully surrendered to Jesus. Resist giving in to feelings of guilt. Remember, Jesus wants your obedience and heart, not perfection. Simply come to Him in this moment and ask, "Jesus, what do you want for me?"

_____

_____

_____

_____

_____

_____

_____

3

BE AN IMITATOR OF GOD

PAUL SAYS TO THE EPHESIANS that we are to "follow God's example . . . as dearly loved children" (Ephesians 5:1). There is a tender scene in *Jaws* (it's true, there is) where Sheriff Brody is sitting at dinner with his young son. As the scene unfolds, the son imitates the movements of his dad. When Brody notices, he begins to play along and is suddenly reminded of who he is, what he needs to do, and who he needs to protect.

As you read Scripture, write down the character traits of God, Jesus, and the Holy Spirit. Pray for opportunities to live out those traits in your life. When we focus on all the good, it leaves less space for anxiety to sneak in.